Original title:
The Empty Chair

Copyright © 2024 Swan Charm
All rights reserved.

Author: Swan Charm
ISBN HARDBACK: 978-9908-1-2617-3
ISBN PAPERBACK: 978-9908-1-2618-0
ISBN EBOOK: 978-9908-1-2619-7

An Invitation to Remember

In twilight's glow, we find the past,
Whispers of moments, forever cast.
Time stands still, like a gentle stream,
Inviting us back to a shared dream.

Beneath the stars, our laughter danced,
Captured in frames, fate's sweet romance.
Each smile a thread, woven so tight,
A tapestry bright, glowing with light.

The echoes of joy, soft as the breeze,
Call us to pause, to take our ease.
In every corner, memories bloom,
Filling the heart, erasing the gloom.

Let us revisit, with tender care,
The moments that linger, the love we share.
With open arms, we gather near,
An invitation to hold what is dear.

So raise a glass to the times we've spent,
To laughter and love, to dreams well-meant.
Together we weave, through shadow and light,
An invitation to remember, shining bright.

A Gaze Towards Yesterday

In the mirror, shadows play,
I see echoes of dismay.
Faded colors, once so bright,
Whisper secrets of the night.

Old photographs, a gentle sigh,
Remind me of days gone by.
Laughing faces in the sun,
A tapestry of what was fun.

Time, the thief, steals away,
Leaving memories in disarray.
Yet in stillness, I can find,
A glimpse of what once intertwined.

With every laugh and every tear,
Yesterday's moments feel so near.
In regrets and dreams I tread,
A gaze reflects the path I've led.

Fleeting Moments

Like petals falling from the tree,
Each moment drifts so silently.
A fleeting glance, a soft embrace,
Time dances in a fragile space.

Sunrise whispers secrets low,
As shadows stretch and ebb like flow.
Laughter rings in the evening air,
Traces left without a care.

The clock ticks on, yet I stand still,
Capturing time with tender will.
Every heartbeat, every sigh,
Moments fade as clouds drift by.

In a blink, we lose our grasp,
Like grains of sand within the clasp.
Yet in their essence, memories bloom,
A bouquet brightens the coming gloom.

The Space Between Words

In silence thick, we find our place,
A language wrapped in soft embrace.
Glimmers shine in every pause,
Sparks of truth without a cause.

Each heartbeat echoes what we feel,
In spoken thoughts our hearts reveal.
Yet more is said in quiet stares,
The sacred bond that love declares.

Words can falter, voices strain,
But silence speaks in joy and pain.
In the depth of unwritten lore,
Resides the heart we can explore.

Moments linger, heavy air,
The weight of meaning everywhere.
In the space where words fall shy,
Understanding lingers nearby.

Conversations in Silence

In whispered looks, our secrets dwell,
Conversations words cannot tell.
A touch, a smile, a knowing glance,
In quietude, our hearts will dance.

The world outside can fade away,
As we find solace in the gray.
Unspoken thoughts, like threads, entwine,
Creating bonds that can align.

Amidst the rush, the noise, the haste,
We carve a space, divine and chaste.
Where silence blooms and feelings rise,
In tranquil depths, love never lies.

Like shadows blending into light,
Our souls connect in soft twilight.
In every pause, a world unfolds,
In conversations, silence holds.

Echoes in Silence

In the stillness, whispers play,
Lost words drift, fade away.
Beneath the moon's soft glow,
Silent tales begin to flow.

Footsteps linger on the floor,
Shadows dance, memories soar.
Time has woven threads of night,
Echoes lost in fading light.

Hearts once bold, now wrapped in gray,
Longing for a brighter day.
Yet in silence, hope remains,
Softly calling through the chains.

A Space Yet Filled

In this room, a light does glow,
Whispers linger soft and low.
Every corner, every space,
Holds a memory's embrace.

Frames adorned with smiles and tears,
Hopes and dreams throughout the years.
Yet between the walls, a sigh,
A promise made, but left to dry.

The air is thick with what was said,
Through the silence, words still tread.
In each breath, a story spun,
A space yet filled, though time has run.

Faded Memories in the Dust

Shadows settle, dust does cling,
Faded echoes gently sing.
Photographs in sepia hues,
Time erases, yet renews.

Cracked frames hold a world once bright,
Moments trapped in fading light.
Forgotten faces, ghostly smiles,
Trace the paths of countless miles.

In the silence, feelings lie,
Whispers of a gentle sigh.
Faded dreams in shadows cast,
Holding on to moments past.

Shadows of What Was

In the twilight, shadows creep,
Remnants of the dreams we keep.
Every corner holds a sigh,
Tales of laughter, tears will dry.

Halls that echo with your name,
Flickers of a mellow flame.
Time has changed the way we see,
But shadows still remember me.

Ghosts of laughter, whispers bright,
Dance in memories of the night.
Through the darkness, light will flow,
Shadows of what was, still glow.

The Pause of Life

Life takes a breath, a gentle sigh,
Moments linger as time slips by.
In quiet corners, thoughts collide,
We find our peace, where dreams reside.

In stillness, echoes softly sound,
In every heartbeat, love is found.
A fleeting glance, a soft embrace,
We hold the now, a sacred space.

Through shadows cast by passing years,
We learn to laugh, we learn to tear.
The pause reveals, our truths defined,
In every silence, life aligned.

The rush may fade, like whispers blown,
In gentle pauses, seeds are sown.
Life's melody, a sweet refrain,
In stillness found, we rise again.

Layers of Longing

Beneath the surface, secrets lie,
In every glance, a silent cry.
With every heartbeat, stories weave,
In layers thick, we learn to grieve.

The depth of longing, bittersweet,
In crowded rooms, we feel complete.
Yet empty spaces, they still call,
A silent echo, a whispered thrall.

We wear our masks, the world can't see,
The hidden layers want to be free.
In tangled dreams, we find our way,
Through shadows deep, we dare to stay.

Each layer peeled, reveals our core,
Embracing all, we become more.
In every heartbeat, there's a song,
A symphony where we belong.

Surrender to Silence

In quietude, the heart will race,
In stillness, find an open space.
Where thoughts dissolve and worries wane,
Surrendering all, we break the chain.

A gentle breeze, a fleeting sound,
In silence deep, our truths are found.
With every breath, the world we know,
Transforms to peace, a gentle flow.

In whispered dreams, we touch the void,
Finding solace where fear's destroyed.
In surrender's arms, we learn to be,
A part of all, an endless sea.

So let the silence embrace our souls,
In every pause, we become whole.
A silent promise, profound and bright,
Surrender to the depth of night.

Whispers of Abandon

In shadows dim, where dreams entwine,
The whispers call, your hand in mine.
Through empty streets, we drift along,
In moments fleeting, we feel so strong.

The thrill of night, the stars align,
In every kiss, a spark divine.
We dance through chaos, wild and free,
In whispered words, we learn to see.

Echoes linger, soft and sweet,
In every heartbeat, the world retreats.
Let go of worries, surrender the fear,
In whispers of abandon, we draw near.

With every glance, a promise new,
In secrets shared, we chase the blue.
In shadows deep, where stories blend,
We find our solace, a timeless mend.

Between the Lines

In shadows and whispers, we find our way,
Words on the page, where thoughts drift and sway.
Between every sentence, a story unfolds,
Silent confessions that language beholds.

Moments unspoken, the glances we share,
Heartbeats in sync, a dance in the air.
Chasing the gaps where intentions reside,
Between every heartbeat, there's nowhere to hide.

Memories linger, like ink on the skin,
Searching for meaning, where dreams can begin.
Written in silence, our truths intertwine,
Between the deep pauses, your heart calls for mine.

A tapestry woven with threads of the night,
Mysteries linger, just out of our sight.
With each subtle gesture, a language we speak,
Between every letter, it's you that I seek.

A Space to Fill

An empty canvas waits, so wide and so bare,
Colors of life dance, creating a flare.
With brush strokes of dreams, the visions take flight,
In a space to fill, we aim for the light.

Echoes of laughter linger in the air,
Whispers of memories, moments we share.
In each little corner, potential resides,
In a space to fill, our passion abides.

Fragments of longing, we paint as we go,
With shades of emotion, our spirits will glow.
Each layer revealing, the stories concealed,
In a space to fill, our hearts are revealed.

Stillness surrounds us, the world fades away,
In the silence, creation starts to play.
With hands intertwined, we'll sketch out the thrill,
In a space to fill, with love as our quill.

Fragments of Longing

In the depths of the night, a longing will rise,
Whispers of dreams dance like stars in the skies.
Scattered in pieces, our hopes start to gleam,
Fragments of longing, woven in a dream.

Notes of a song drift from far-off places,
Echoes of laughter in familiar faces.
Searching for solace in moments untold,
Fragments of longing wrapped gently in gold.

Paths that we wander, though distant they seem,
Lead back to each other, a sweet common theme.
In every heartbeat, the pull, it is strong,
Fragments of longing, where we both belong.

Yet, time remains fickle, elusive and shy,
Catching our wishes as they whisper by.
In the stillness of night, our spirits will sing,
Fragments of longing, together take wing.

Echoes of Familiarity

In crowded rooms, where laughter rings clear,
Familiar faces weave stories sincere.
Each glance a reminder of moments once shared,
Echoes of familiarity, lives that we've bared.

The warmth of old tales wraps softly around,
In the tapestry woven, connection is found.
Through trials and triumphs, we learn to embrace,
Echoes of familiarity, our safe, cherished space.

We speak without words, a knowing so deep,
In silence, a treasure, our secrets we keep.
Through chapters of time, we dance and we sway,
Echoes of familiarity lead us each day.

With every shared memory, new paths we'll create,
In the heart of the moment, our spirits elate.
For in every heartbeat, a memory gleams,
Echoes of familiarity, the fabric of dreams.

A Shadow's Farewell

In the twilight's gentle breath,
A shadow whispers goodbye,
Fading into the soft night,
With stars lighting the sky.

Memories linger like smoke,
As the echoes start to fade,
Each moment held in silence,
In the stillness, I wade.

What was once bright and bold,
Now dims in the evening glow,
But in the heart, it stays warm,
A light none can overthrow.

The past is a haunting song,
Each note a fleeting embrace,
Yet in the shadows, I find,
A comfort in this space.

So I bid a soft farewell,
To the shadows of today,
For in every end, a start,
A new dawn on the way.

Vestiges of Togetherness

In the quiet of our days,
Where laughter used to bloom,
I find the traces of us,
In the corners of a room.

Echoes of shared whispers,
Dance softly on the air,
Each moment like a ribbon,
Woven with tender care.

Time weaves a gentle veil,
Over what once was clear,
Yet the feelings remain strong,
As if you are still near.

Photographs of laughter,
Caught in a fleeting glance,
Remind me of the beauty,
In love's enduring dance.

Though paths may diverge ahead,
Our stories intertwine,
In the heart's sacred space,
Your spirit will still shine.

Stillness with Hope

In the stillness of the night,
Hope flickers like a flame,
Guiding through the shadows,
Whispering a name.

The world rests in silence,
Cradled in moonlight's grace,
Each breath a soft promise,
A moment to embrace.

Stars twinkle above,
In an endless, velvet sea,
Reminding me of dreams,
That visit quietly.

In the depths of my heart,
A new dawn starts to swell,
Wrapped in the warmth of faith,
In this stillness, all is well.

So I cling to the quiet,
With the dawn's soft embrace,
For in stillness, there is hope,
In this sacred space.

Unseen Presence

In the room where you once stood,
An unseen presence looms,
A whisper in the shadows,
Filling up the rooms.

Though I cannot touch you,
Your spirit lingers near,
In the laughter echoing,
In the memories held dear.

The scent of your essence,
Dances in the air,
In every quiet corner,
I find comfort everywhere.

Time has a gentle way,
Of blending past with now,
In shadows, I still see you,
In each and every vow.

You are the unseen warmth,
In the silence of my days,
A presence felt within,
In so many little ways.

The Weight of Stillness

In shadows cast by time's embrace,
Each breath, a gentle sigh of space.
Whispers linger in the air,
A heartbeat's weight, a silent care.

The clock ticks softly, moments stall,
In every second, echoes call.
The world stands still, a fleeting dream,
While stillness wraps in muted theme.

Beneath the sky, a canvas wide,
A weight to bear, a place to hide.
In solitude, the heart can find,
A solace deep, a peace entwined.

Yet in the hush, what truths arise,
In quietness, the spirit flies.
The weight of stillness, sweet and stark,
Reveals the light within the dark.

A Corner of Longing

In corners where the shadows creep,
A longing stirs, a promise deep.
Forgotten dreams on dusty shelves,
Whispers of what we once called selves.

The heartbeats echo, soft but clear,
In every sigh, a silent tear.
Memories woven into the night,
A flicker of hope, a distant light.

Beyond the veil of what we crave,
A canvas painted, the heart's own wave.
In every corner, stories hide,
Longing, a river, forever wide.

And so we stand in twilight's hue,
Chasing shadows, longing anew.
In that corner, dreams take flight,
A place of wishes, woven bright.

Threads of Yesterday

In woven tapestries of time,
Threads of yesterday softly chime.
Colors blend, a story spun,
Each moment lived, a battle won.

The past, a garden rich and wild,
Echoes of laughter, dreams defiled.
Stitches hidden, tales unsaid,
In every thread, the path we tread.

Yet in the fabric, hope's embrace,
A thread of light, a sacred space.
Binding us to all we've known,
In every fiber, we have grown.

Tomorrow waits, a canvas bare,
With threads of yesterday in the air.
A journey onward, we shall weave,
In every heartbeat, we believe.

Solitary Silence

In solitary silence, shadows dwell,
A quiet echo, a whispered shell.
The world drifts by, a distant song,
In stillness found, where hearts belong.

The moonlight spills on empty streets,
In solitude, the spirit meets.
Whispers dance like leaves in flight,
A secret shared with the soft night.

The stars above, a scattered scroll,
Guide the wanderer, seek the soul.
In silence forged, a bond is made,
A friend to keep when dreams do fade.

Yet in the hush, strength is born,
From solitude, a new dawn worn.
In solitary silence, we find grace,
A gentle heart, a sacred place.

The Unseen Presence

In shadows deep where whispers fade,
A figure stands, yet not displayed.
With gentle sighs, it fills the room,
An echo of a past that looms.

It breathes in silence, soft and low,
A warmth that only hearts can know.
In fleeting glances, it resides,
In every tear and every tide.

Forgotten dreams hang in the air,
Its presence lingers, everywhere.
Like moonlight dancing on the floor,
A reminder of the evermore.

We search for signs, to understand,
This unseen force, a guiding hand.
Though eyes may fail to see the soul,
Its touch remains, it makes us whole.

So let us cherish what we find,
In gentle whispers, intertwined.
For love does not know bounds or space,
In every heart, it leaves its trace.

Ghosts of Conversations Past

In corners dark, they softly speak,
Of laughter shared, and futures bleak.
Their voices wander, fade, and swell,
In stories only time can tell.

Each word a ghost, a fleeting breath,
Reminders of both life and death.
With echoes sharp, they ring in me,
The lessons learned, the lost and free.

They linger still, these shades of night,
In memories that hold us tight.
Each pause and sigh, a bittersweet,
A tapestry of love complete.

As dawn approaches, shadows wane,
Yet still they haunt, like summer rain.
In every moment, lost or found,
Their whispers wrap the heart unbound.

So let us cherish voices clear,
The ghosts of love, forever near.
For in our hearts, they will remain,
Through joy and sorrow, loss and gain.

A Seat Left Vacant

At the table set for two,
One chair stands empty, just for you.
In silence, echoes start to play,
Of laughter shared and words we'd say.

The candle flickers, shadows dance,
Remind me of our fleeting chance.
Your favorite drink, still in the glass,
A toast to moments, now surpassed.

This space remains, a solemn bond,
A seat left vacant, memory's fond.
With every meal, I taste the ache,
Of all the dreams that time could break.

Though time will pass, this chair stays put,
In every gathering, thoughts take root.
A ghostly presence, sweet yet sad,
In every memory, the good and bad.

So here I sit with heart in hand,
With hope that love will understand.
For though you're gone, I'll hold this place,
A tribute to your warm embrace.

The Echo of Absence

In silent rooms where shadows linger,
The echo calls, a subtle singer.
Each whispered thought, a fading sigh,
Of all the times we said goodbye.

The walls absorb the tales we spun,
In laughter bright, in light we run.
Yet silence falls, a heavy shroud,
As absence wraps me like a cloud.

I search for traces, faint and dim,
Where light once danced, now shadows skim.
The echo of your voice remains,
A melody that holds my pains.

In dreams, you speak, a fleeting ghost,
A presence felt, what hurts the most.
But waking brings the truth, the pain,
The echo's sweet, but leaves its stain.

So I will carry what we had,
In every joy, in every sad.
For in this heart, your song will play,
An echo of love that will not stray.

Unraveled Threads of Time

In the fabric of the night, they fray,
Whispers of memories drift away.
Colors fade, the edges torn,
Dreams and hopes, too soon reborn.

A tapestry of moments lost,
Each thread a tale, a heavy cost.
Woven paths that twist and turn,
Lessons learned, yet still we yearn.

The clock ticks on, relentless chime,
Echoes of laughter, faces in rhyme.
In shadows where the past resides,
Time unspools as each heart hides.

Gathered fragments, silently shared,
In this maze, no one has cared.
Yet still we seek that golden light,
To mend the threads deep in the night.

A Lonely Gathering Spot

Underneath the old oak tree,
Ghosts of laughter, wild and free.
Empty benches, tales untold,
Memories linger, growing cold.

Footprints in the dust remain,
Traces left of joy and pain.
A flicker of the past's embrace,
In solitude, we find our place.

Leaves whisper secrets on the ground,
In this haven, peace is found.
Sitting still, the world will pass,
Moments captured, like shards of glass.

Beneath the stars, a watchful night,
Gathering shadows, soft and slight.
Here I ponder what has been,
In quiet corners, dreams grow thin.

Unfamiliar Company in Stillness

In the silence, voices hum,
Echoes of thoughts, feelings numb.
Presence felt, though none in sight,
Whispers dance like moths in flight.

Shadows stretch across the floor,
Familiar faces, yet no more.
Each glance a story left behind,
In this stillness, we're entwined.

Finding solace in the void,
In this quiet, heartbeats cloyed.
A silent pact, a bond unspoken,
In the stillness, hearts awakened.

Time stands still, and moments freeze,
Company found in the gentle breeze.
Together here, though worlds apart,
In stillness, we stitch the heart.

A Place Where Dreams Once Sat

Where shadows grew in the fading light,
Dreams would whisper through the night.
Once a haven, now but dust,
A hollow shell of fading trust.

Memories linger in the air,
Echoes of hopes, beyond compare.
Farewell laughter, a soft refrain,
In these corners, only pain.

The sunlight filters through the cracks,
Painting pictures of what it lacks.
Once vibrant scenes now faded gray,
In this space, the dreams decay.

Yet still, I wander, searching deep,
In the silence, memories sleep.
A fragile thread connects us all,
In this place where dreams once sprawled.

The Loneliness of Space

Stars whisper softly in the night,
But silence prevails in their flight.
Planets drift through the endless tide,
Lonely shadows cannot hide.

Vastness stretches beyond the eye,
Dreams and hopes in the void lie.
Comets race with a fleeting grace,
Yet none can solve this empty space.

Galaxies swirl, a dance so grand,
Yet isolation, a heavy hand.
Between the worlds, a chill does cling,
To the echoes that silence brings.

In the silence where wonders bloom,
Loneliness finds its room.
Cosmic tales left to unfold,
In the void, pure and cold.

What whispers linger in the dark?
What mysteries spark the heart?
In the abyss, a haunting chase,
Forever lost, the loneliest space.

Echoing Footsteps

Down the hall, a sound resounds,
Faint echoes stir where silence bounds.
Each footfall tells a story past,
Of moments lived, shadows cast.

In empty rooms, their whispers carry,
Memories linger, bittersweet and wary.
A gentle creak of weathered wood,
Recalls the laughter that once stood.

Every stride through the silent air,
Calls forth the souls who once were there.
Each step a note in a ghostly song,
Resounding where they still belong.

The echo fades into the night,
As time erases once-bright light.
Yet in the stillness, hearts do know,
The warmth of love will always flow.

So let the footsteps softly tread,
In the spaces where we've fled.
For echoes hold what hearts once told,
In time, both hushed and bold.

Dust on the Cushion

On the couch where we used to sit,
Time has settled, memories knit.
Dust collects where laughter rang,
In the stillness, silence hangs.

Cushions worn from love's embrace,
Each mark a memory, a gentle trace.
Faint whispers of your soft sighs,
In the quiet, the heart replies.

Sunlight filters through the gloom,
Highlighting all that we presume.
A spectral trace of what was there,
Ghostly echoes fill the air.

Yet in the dust, a warmth remains,
A bond unbroken by time's reigns.
Though moments fade like fleeting bliss,
In quiet corners, love still exists.

So let the dust blanket the space,
Where once we shared time's tender grace.
For every speck tells a tale true,
Of the life that once bloomed anew.

Stories Left Untold

In the corners where shadows dwell,
Lie stories wrapped in a silent shell.
Words unspoken, dreams left bare,
In the stillness, they linger there.

The pages turned, but never read,
Tales of light and whispers of dread.
Every heartbeat holds a line,
Of moments lost that intertwine.

In the quiet, a beckoning call,
Ancient echoes in faded hall.
History waits in a fleeting glance,
Wishing for its change to dance.

Yet in each heart, they softly weep,
For secrets buried deep in sleep.
Hopes and fears left to unfold,
In the spaces where they are told.

So gather close to the stories missed,
Embrace the shadows that twist.
For every tale that time has held,
Is a journey waiting to be spelled.

The Chair That Remains

In the corner, shadows play,
An empty chair where you would stay.
Dust gathers, silence prevails,
Memories linger, like ghostly tales.

Fabric frayed, it's worn with time,
Once held laughter, joy, and rhyme.
Now it whispers in quiet tones,
The echo of love, a heart that moans.

Seated still, in the fading light,
Hopes and dreams take flight, then bite.
The evening passes, time won't wait,
Yet the chair remains, a silent fate.

Last embrace, a fleeting glance,
Life moves on, a fleeting chance.
Yet here it stays, through day and night,
Holding shadows, holding light.

Years will flow, yet it won't break,
A witness to love, a heartache.
In this chair, a piece of soul,
An empty space that can't be whole.

Ghostly Connections

Whispers weave through the air,
Ghostly echoes everywhere.
A touch, a breath, a fleeting glance,
In rooms where shadows twist and dance.

Threads of time bind us tight,
In the dark, we find the light.
Unseen bonds that pull and sway,
Carrying hearts that drift away.

Voices rise from the dust of days,
Softly guiding through the haze.
Old stories linger, never fade,
In the silence, connections made.

A chill runs down your spine at night,
Presence felt, a spark of fright.
Yet in this space, love still flows,
In ghostly realms where no one knows.

Hands once held now touch the air,
With memories too sweet to bear.
As night draws close and spirits sway,
Ghostly connections, here to stay.

Remains of a Gathering

Cups and chairs, the laughter's seed,
In this space, we plant a need.
Echoes of joy in vacant halls,
Faded footsteps, familiar calls.

Photographs hang on the wall,
Frozen moments, time's sweet thrall.
The table set for stories old,
An untold warmth, memories bold.

We gathered close, in smiles and tears,
Sharing tales spanning years.
Yet now the silence drapes like lace,
In the aftermath, we find our place.

Sunlight fades, shadows creep,
In the stillness, secrets keep.
Remains of laughter, whispers' song,
In absence felt, we still belong.

Empty chairs beneath the glow,
A silent promise, love won't go.
Though time may pass and gatherings cease,
In the heart remains a piece.

An Untold Story in Silence

Whispers linger where words don't go,
In the quiet, secrets flow.
The weight of thoughts, a heavy shroud,
In silence loud, emotions proud.

Eyes that speak, yet lips are sealed,
An untold story, fate revealed.
Each glance a chapter, each breath a line,
In the hush, our hearts entwine.

Beneath the stars, where dreams reside,
In quiet moments, love won't hide.
A canvas blank, a tale unfolds,
With silent depth, its warmth it holds.

In shadows cast and twilight's gleam,
Lives entwined in a silent dream.
With every pause, a universe grows,
In unspoken words, true love shows.

So let the silence weave its thread,
In every heartbeat, words left unsaid.
An untold story, a whisper's might,
In the stillness, we find our light.

Hollow Haven

In the depths of fading light,
Whispers linger in the air,
Echoes of a lost delight,
Silent shadows, unaware.

Cracked walls hold forgotten dreams,
Dust dances in a ghostly way,
Hope slips through like fragile beams,
Vanishing with the light of day.

A memory etched in the stone,
Chilling breezes, hushed and cold,
A place where hearts once called home,
Now stands silent, worn and old.

Footsteps fade upon the floor,
Softly tracing love's last song,
Hollow, yet it yearns for more,
Where the echoes still belong.

In the hush, the stories weave,
Time encapsulated here,
Yet in the stillness I believe,
Life once thrived, so bright and clear.

Where Shadows Gather

Beneath the boughs, the shadows play,
They twist and twine in evening's grace,
A dance of night, they softly sway,
   In secret corners, they embrace.

Time slows down in twilight's clutch,
As whispers blend with rustling leaves,
Here every moment holds its touch,
   In mysteries that dusk conceives.

Hidden hearts in twilight bloom,
They share their dreams, yet stay concealed,
In the soft and shadowed room,
   Silent promises revealed.

Where light dares not to tread with pride,
The past meets present, calm yet wild,
In the embrace of night confide,
   For in this veil, the lost are riled.

When shadows gather, fears unspool,
We weave the tales of days gone by,
In the darkness, we find our pool,
Where hopes and memories never die.

Unoccupied Silence

In corners where the dust collects,
Time holds its breath, a ceaseless wait,
Echoes of laughter, now defects,
In vacant rooms, we contemplate.

Walls that once hummed with our dreams,
Now whisper low, a mournful tune,
Through empty halls, a stillness gleams,
Beneath the watchful gaze of moon.

As shadows stretch, the night unfolds,
Each crack reveals a story splayed,
In silence, ancient truths are told,
In this void, memories cascade.

Yet even voids are filled with light,
A promise rests in each still space,
We breathe in sorrow, then take flight,
In unoccupied, we find grace.

The heart remembers what the eyes roam,
In silence, love's soft words abide,
A place that's empty, yet feels like home,
Where we find peace, and time can't hide.

Remnants of Togetherness

In sepia tones, our laughter stays,
Faded photos tell tales of old,
Sunlit moments, in gentle rays,
Of the warmth that love once sold.

Weaving threads of memory bright,
In the fabric of days once shared,
Each stitch holds whispers of delight,
In shadows where our hearts declared.

Of sunsets watched, of dreams pursued,
In every glance, a spark ignites,
Even in parting, love accrued,
In the silence, our bond ignites.

Time may stretch and paths may part,
Yet the heart knows no divide,
For in each piece, we bear our art,
Together, even worlds collide.

In remnants, love's soft glow remains,
A testament to what once bloomed,
Through laughter, heartache, joy, and pains,
In every echo, we've resumed.

A Timeless Pause

In the hush of dawn's first light,
Moments linger, soft and bright.
A whisper rides the gentle breeze,
Encased in silence, time's reprieve.

Clocks stand still, the world holds breath,
Caught in the tender hands of rest.
Each tick a ghost, each tock a sigh,
As dreams weave softly, drawing nigh.

The sun spills gold on dew-kissed grass,
Painting memories that will not pass.
A pause, a glance, a fleeting thought,
In every heartbeat, beauty caught.

Beneath the boughs where shadows play,
Time winks at us in its ballet.
We sip the stillness, taste the air,
In this embrace, we find our care.

With every moment made to last,
We gather whispers from the past.
In timeless pause, we seek and find,
The threads that bind both heart and mind.

Preserved in Air

A breath away, the echoes cling,
Of laughter lost and fleeting spring.
In golden hues, the memories soar,
Preserved in air, forevermore.

Fleeting shadows dance with grace,
In twilight's arms, they find their place.
With gentle sighs, the dusk unfolds,
As time's soft stories whisper old.

Petals drift on currents rare,
Their fragrance mingled with the air.
Each note a timeline, finely spun,
Of days remembered, tales begun.

The world around us, vast and wide,
Carries whispers where we bide.
In every rustle, every sigh,
The ghosts of yesteryears draw nigh.

So let us linger in this space,
Where memories bloom with every trace.
For in this stillness, we believe,
Time's gentle gift, our hearts receive.

The Seat of Memories

A creaky chair by the old oak tree,
Holds whispers of who we used to be.
In sunlight's warm embrace, we sit,
With echoes of laughter, timeless wit.

Worn wood cradles the tales untold,
Of summers enjoyed and dreams bold.
Each splintered line, a story shared,
In its presence, we're always paired.

The breeze carries secrets, soft and clear,
Of moments cherished and held dear.
In the seat of memories, we reside,
With love and longing, side by side.

Time weaves around us in gentle threads,
Holding us close, where memory spreads.
In silent pauses, we find our way,
Guided by love, come what may.

So take a seat, let's reminisce,
In this refuge, a timeless bliss.
Together, always, in heart and mind,
In the seat of memories, peace we find.

When Time Stood Still

A moment captured in twilight's glow,
When time stood still, hearts felt the flow.
Each glance exchanged beneath the sky,
Held the world gently, you and I.

The air was thick with unspoken words,
As silence sang like gentle birds.
In that stillness, with soft caress,
We found a haven, sweet with rest.

Stars danced above, a radiant plume,
In dreams of warmth, we found our bloom.
Each heartbeat echoed, a timeless song,
In this embrace, we both belong.

The universe paused as we drew near,
In every sigh, in every tear.
Moments unveiled, wrapped in a thrill,
Whispered softly: time stood still.

In the quiet, we carved our space,
Two souls entwined in timeless grace.
For in that instant, calm and bright,
We painted forever with love's pure light.

Sanctuary of Reflection

In the quiet of night, I find peace,
Whispers of dreams begin to cease.
Shadows dance softly on the wall,
Here in my heart, I hear their call.

Thoughts like whispers, gentle and light,
Filling the void, embracing the night.
Memories linger, sweet and bittersweet,
In this haven, I find my heartbeat.

Nature's embrace, the rustling leaves,
In this space, my spirit retrieves.
Stars above like diamonds shine,
Guiding my soul, the path divine.

Water's murmur, the moon's soft gleam,
Cradling my heart in a woven dream.
Time stands still as I breathe it in,
Finding solace where I begin.

Here in silence, truths unfold,
Stories of life that softly told.
Beneath the surface, wisdom flows,
In this sanctuary, my spirit grows.

An Unspoken Bond

In the laughter shared beneath the stars,
Silent messages travel, without bars.
Eyes that meet speak a thousand tales,
In this connection, love never fails.

Hands entwined, warmth in the chill,
No words are needed, hearts can still.
Glimpses of joy in a fleeting glance,
In this unspoken bond, we dance.

Through trials faced and storms we've weathered,
In quiet moments, our souls are tethered.
Language unspoken, yet deeply known,
In the space between us, seeds are sown.

Through time and distance, we remain near,
In uncharted pathways, we conquer fear.
The bond we share is a timeless thread,
In every silence, our love is fed.

With every heartbeat, stronger we grow,
A force of nature, a gentle flow.
In this sacred space, we find our way,
An unspoken bond, come what may.

Buzz of Forgotten Laughter

Echoes of joy in the empty halls,
Memories linger in the silent calls.
Laughter that danced on air like light,
Now whispers softly, fading from sight.

Childhood days wrapped in warm embrace,
Graphics of time on an ageless face.
Each giggle a story, a moment in flight,
Now just shadows in the deepening night.

Friends like stars, scattered afar,
Yet in my heart, they remain, ajar.
The buzz of laughter, a distant sound,
In the stillness, its essence found.

Time may change the shape of the scene,
Yet in those echoes, we're always seen.
A treasure of moments held so tight,
Buzz of forgotten laughter, pure delight.

In nostalgia's warmth, we dwell for a while,
In fleeting memories, life brings a smile.
Though time may pass, and we drift apart,
Laughter's soft echo lives in the heart.

Space Where You Sat

In the corner where sunlight spills,
A vacant chair, the heart it fills.
An imprint left from moments shared,
In this space, so much has cared.

Your laughter lingers, a gentle trace,
In memories woven, I find my place.
The warmth of your spirit, a fragrant bloom,
In this small corner, love finds room.

Faded echoes of stories told,
In silence, your presence still feels bold.
Time may have passed, but this remains,
A sacred space, where love sustains.

I close my eyes, and there you are,
In dreams, your light shines from afar.
This space where you sat holds us both,
A testament to love, a cherished oath.

Here in the quiet, I hold you close,
In every heartbeat, your memory flows.
Though space may change, one thing stays true,
In this sacred corner, I'm always with you.

The Watchful Gaze

In shadows deep, a watchful eye,
Observes the night as stars drift by.
Silent and still, a world unfolds,
In whispered tales and secrets told.

A flicker here, a rustle there,
The quiet dance of twilight's air.
Each moment etched in fleeting time,
A silent witness, thoughts sublime.

With bated breath, the dawn will break,
The watchful gaze will never shake.
Through every dusk and every dawn,
Eternal guardian, never gone.

In hidden corners where shadows play,
It lingers on, come what may.
A sentinel of life's embrace,
The watchful heart, a timeless grace.

So heed the gaze that knows your soul,
In every crack, it finds a whole.
For in the silence, it resides,
The watchful gaze that never hides.

Sifting Through Silence

In the hush of night, thoughts collide,
Sifting through silence, where dreams reside.
Whispers of truth in shadows cast,
Echoes of moments, fading fast.

Each flicker of light breaks the dark,
A gentle nudge, a tender spark.
Thoughts woven soft in twilight's veil,
Carrying secrets of a quiet tale.

The heart beats slow, a steady drum,
As silence hums a waiting strum.
Between each pause, life breathes anew,
In sifting silence, I find you.

Each layer peeled, a story bare,
In fleeting whispers, memories share.
The quiet dance, a moments' bliss,
In sifting through silence, this is bliss.

So linger here, let worries cease,
In tranquil hush, we find our peace.
Together we'll weave the night's embrace,
Sifting through silence, time's gentle grace.

Points of Connection

In the web of life, threads intertwine,
Points of connection, clear and divine.
A glance exchanged, a smile so bright,
Infinite bonds, in morning light.

From heart to heart, the journey flows,
Like rivers streaming, love always grows.
In laughter shared, we find our ground,
With every moment, solace found.

In crowded rooms, or quiet parks,
Each touch we share ignites new sparks.
Invisible lines draw us near,
In every connection, the world feels clear.

In differences found, we learn to see,
That points of connection set us free.
A tapestry woven with loves embrace,
In points of connection, we find our place.

So cherish the ties that bind and hold,
Each story shared, a tale untold.
In every heartbeat, a world to explore,
Points of connection, forevermore.

Whispers of the Past

Echoes of memories softly sigh,
Whispers of the past that never die.
In the autumn leaves that dance and spin,
Stories once cherished, tucked within.

Fragments of laughter, shadows of pain,
In the folds of time, they still remain.
Each fleeting moment, a delicate trace,
Whispers of the past, a warm embrace.

Through dusty pages and faded ink,
In every silence, we pause and think.
Of paths once traveled under starlit skies,
Whispers of the past, where memory lies.

With every heartbeat, history calls,
In gentle tones, as twilight falls.
We gather the pieces, both lost and found,
Whispers of the past, a sacred sound.

So let us listen, let us hold near,
The echoes of laughter, the remnants of fear.
In the tapestry woven, we find the strength,
Whispers of the past, a timeless length.

Silent Sentinel

In shadows deep, the watchful gaze,
A guardian's heart through endless days.
Unyielding strength, though silent and still,
Amidst the night, a steadfast will.

Beneath the moon, the secrets lie,
Whispers carried on winds that sigh.
Time drifts slowly, yet here I stand,
A beacon bright on forgotten land.

Through storms that roar and darkness near,
I hold the light, I feel no fear.
For in the quiet, strength is found,
A promised hope in hallowed ground.

With every breath, I weave a thread,
Of all the dreams and words unsaid.
In silence, stories start to grow,
As time flows gently, soft and slow.

So linger close, my watchful friend,
Together we will find the end.
In silence wrapped, we shall abide,
Through eternal nights, a loyal guide.

Ghost in the Corner

In quiet rooms where shadows play,
A whisper soft, a hint of gray.
Lingering echoes of what once was,
A fleeting touch, a silent pause.

In empty chairs, a presence glows,
Faint reminders of love that grows.
A ghostly sigh in twilight's breath,
Revealing tales of life and death.

Windows rattle, dust motes dance,
Fleeting glimpses of half a chance.
In the corners where silence falls,
A spirit waits and softly calls.

Through veils of time and space apart,
It's woven deep inside my heart.
Though I can't see, I know it's there,
A gentle ghost, forever rare.

When dusk descends, I feel the pull,
Of memories bright and beautiful.
In the shadows, I am not alone,
For every corner leads me home.

Absent Embrace

In the stillness, I reach for you,
But empty air my fingers woo.
An absent touch, a longing sigh,
In dreams, we dance, yet wake to cry.

The warmth we shared now drifts away,
Like autumn leaves on winds that sway.
Each moment passed, a hollow ache,
In spaces where memories awake.

Through silent nights, I wear the pain,
Of love unspent, like falling rain.
A fleeting glance, a whispered name,
What once was bright, now feels like shame.

Yet in this void, I'll find the light,
A spark of hope in endless night.
For absence gives the heart its worth,
As love transcends the bounds of earth.

So I will hold you, though apart,
In every beat, you fill my heart.
Your essence flows through all I do,
An absent embrace, forever true.

Memories Unsettled

In corners dark, the shadows creep,
A tale of old, through time, I keep.
Whispers linger, echoes chime,
Of moments lost within the rhyme.

Each fragment bright, a puzzle piece,
Of joy and sorrow, never cease.
Through troubled waters, thoughts may sail,
Unraveling dreams in fragile veil.

Beneath the surface, feelings churn,
A restless heart; it yearns to learn.
Threads of laughter, glimmers of tears,
Weaving together the passing years.

In photographs, the smiles reside,
Preserved in time, where love won't hide.
Yet shadows whisper of what's been lost,
A reminder soft of the heavy cost.

So I embrace the unsettled flow,
For through each trial, I will grow.
With open heart, I face the night,
In memory's grasp, I'll find the light.

The Memory Imprint

Faded photographs in a dusty frame,
Whispers of laughter, a soft, sweet name.
Time holds the secrets, it keeps them tight,
In shadows of longing, amidst the night.

Moments like footprints on shifting sand,
Echoes of love only we understand.
The heart clings to echoes, it yearns and sighs,
Dancing with ghosts beneath starry skies.

A fragrance of flowers we used to share,
Old stories told in the midnight air.
Each heartbeat a reminder, each sigh a thread,
Weaving the fabric of words unsaid.

Beneath the still surface, the ripples play,
Memories whisper, then slowly drift away.
Yet in our dreams, they shimmer and glow,
Like embers of fire in the moonlight's flow.

In the quiet moments, they softly gleam,
The memory imprint, a haunting dream.
Through seasons of life, as the years unwind,
We cherish the moments forever enshrined.

The Lost Dialogue

Once we spoke freely beneath the moon,
Now silence lingers, a haunting tune.
Words unspoken float in the air,
Echoes of love, of dreams laid bare.

Conversations woven with threads of gold,
Stories of warmth in the winter cold.
But time drew a curtain, a shadowed veil,
Leaving us stranded with words, frail and pale.

In the stillness grows what we left behind,
An uncharted path that's hard to find.
I search for your voice in the softest breeze,
Yet only the echoes of 'if onlys' tease.

How can we bridge this widening space,
Where silence has taken the sweetest place?
Though distance creates a profound divide,
In dreams, our dialogues still collide.

Our hearts remember what tongues forget,
In the heartbeat of time, we often fret.
Yet hope lingers on, like a flickering flame,
Awaiting the moment we speak once again.

A Specter at Dusk

As daylight wanes into twilight's grasp,
A specter rises from shadows, so fast.
It wanders the fields where wildflowers sway,
Lost in visions of the fading day.

Ghostly whispers weave through the trees,
Carried on the soft, haunting breeze.
A shimmer of light, but a fleeting glance,
The dusk holds secrets, a spectral dance.

With the colors fading to deepening night,
The specter glides with an ethereal light.
It watches the world with a gentle sigh,
As stars awaken in the vast, dark sky.

In moments of stillness, it beckons thee,
To remember the love that forever will be.
With every heartbeat, it draws you near,
A symphony played on the strings of fear.

In the embrace of dusk, it finds its peace,
As whispered promises flow and cease.
In the quiet shadows, the spirits roam,
A specter at dusk, forever home.

Remains of the Day

When the sun dips low, and shadows elongate,
The remnants of daylight hesitate.
In hues of amber and crimson play,
We gather the moments, the remains of the day.

Stories untold in the fading light,
Whispers of dreams that took flight.
As daylight retreats, the night draws near,
We embrace what lingers, what we hold dear.

Each sunset a canvas, each dusk a sigh,
Painting the memories that flutter and fly.
We linger in twilight, hearts in dismay,
Collecting the remnants, the gold hues of gray.

Like grains of sand slipping through our hands,
Time weaves our tales, with swift, subtle strands.
Yet in this stillness, we find our way,
Home in the warmth of the remains of the day.

As stars ignite in the velvet dome,
We cherish the echoes, the feeling of home.
With hearts intertwined, we shall stay,
Forever embracing the remains of the day.

Unheld Conversations

Whispers dance in empty air,
Words unspoken, secrets bare.
Eyes that meet but never stay,
Lingering thoughts, fading away.

In the silence, echoes fade,
Promises lost, plans betrayed.
Moments missed, a fleeting chance,
Dreams that linger, quiet glance.

Time drifts on like drifting leaves,
In the heart, where sorrow weaves.
Unheld tales that fill the void,
Fragile hopes that we avoided.

Shadows stretch and softly sigh,
Unsaid truths that ask us why.
In these spaces, we remain,
Chasing after unheld pain.

Yet in silence, sparks may glow,
In the dark, what we don't show.
A chance to speak, to bridge the gap,
To rewrite words within the map.

A Resting Place for Memories

In the attic of my mind,
Dusty boxes left behind.
Photographs in faded light,
Whisper tales of pure delight.

Every corner, shadows stay,
Silent witnesses to play.
Ticking clocks that once would chime,
Marking moments lost in time.

Breezes carry scents of old,
Fragments of a life retold.
Gentle laughter, echoes clear,
In this place, I hold you near.

A resting place for loves once known,
In my heart, they've gladly grown.
Fleeting glances, summer's sun,
With each breath, they just begun.

In these thoughts, I find my peace,
Memories that never cease.
In every smile and sweet embrace,
A sacred, warm, familiar space.

Absence in the Afternoon Light

Golden beams through windows flow,
Casting shadows, soft and slow.
An empty chair, a quiet sigh,
In the sun, where dreams lie.

Colors fade as daylight wanes,
Lingering thoughts, ghostly chains.
Moments shared that drift away,
In this light, I yearn and stay.

Footsteps echo in my mind,
Whispers of what's left behind.
The warmth of sun, an empty space,
Absence feels a tight embrace.

Evening calls with tender grace,
Yet the light cannot replace.
A silence swells within the glow,
A haunting ache that will not go.

Through the windows, time retreats,
In this quiet, my heart beats.
Between the light and shades of blue,
I find the shade that speaks of you.

Yearning in Unoccupied Spaces

Wide open fields, a gentle breeze,
Rustling leaves upon the trees.
Empty benches, cracked with age,
Sit and ponder, turn the page.

Footpaths worn by passing feet,
In the stillness, dreams compete.
Every shadow, every sigh,
Yearning for what passes by.

A playground swings, deserted now,
Echoes of laughter, a solemn vow.
Time demands the heart to roam,
In these spaces, we feel alone.

Vacant homes, the walls still speak,
Memories linger, bittersweet.
In the silence, hopes arise,
Flickering like distant skies.

Yet in absence, seeds align,
In the quiet, I seek a sign.
Yearning deep in unoccupied places,
With every heartbeat, life embraces.

The Space Between Us

In silence we drift, two worlds apart,
A vast void stretches, a heavy heart.
Words unspoken, feelings unknown,
Yet shadows linger where love once shone.

Promises whispered in twilight's embrace,
Caught in the echoes, a delicate chase.
Fingers reach out, but they never touch,
The space between us, it hurts so much.

Time ticks slowly, with each passing day,
The distance between us, a silent ballet.
Pictures we painted now fade into gray,
The beauty once there seems to drift away.

Memories haunt in soft, gentle streams,
Carried by wind, like forgotten dreams.
In the stillness of night, I'm lost in thought,
Of all the love that we once sought.

Yet hope flickers, a flame in the night,
Can we bridge this chasm, find our light?
In the space between us, love waits so true,
With every heartbeat, I'm longing for you.

A Chair with No Sitter

This chair stands empty, a witness to loss,
Once filled with laughter, now pays the cost.
Its arms remember the warmth of a smile,
But time has taken the joy for a while.

Dust settles softly on the cushion's seam,
Once it embraced, now it's only a dream.
Echoes of conversations hang in the air,
Beneath the silence, a soul laid bare.

The wood creaks softly with memories past,
Each groan a reminder that nothing can last.
Though vacant its place, love lingers still,
In heartbeats and whispers, a warmth to fill.

Windows let in the soft morning light,
Yet shadows remind me of that empty sight.
This chair stands alone, a monument true,
To moments we cherished, to me and to you.

A chair with no sitter, it waits and it sighs,
For the laughter, the stories, the love that won't die.
Find me again, in the warmth of your glow,
Together once more, let the memories flow.

The Shadow of What Might Have Been

In the twilight of dreams we never embraced,
Hearts filled with wishes, memories replaced.
The shadow of choices, so heavy and long,
A whisper of fate in a melancholic song.

Paths that were chosen, now paved with regret,
Time holds the answers we struggle to get.
With each passing moment, my heart calls to you,
In the shadows of time, we once brightly flew.

What if we danced in the glow of the stars?
What if we healed all our old, aching scars?
This shadow reminds me of the love we lost,
Sacrifices made, but what was the cost?

Ghosts of our laughter drift softly in space,
In the echoes of time, I still see your face.
Yet shadows remain, a haunting refrain,
Of all the futures turned into pain.

But in every heartbeat, a flicker persists,
A whisper of hope in the midst of the mist.
Though the shadow of what might have been stays,
In my heart, there's light that forever displays.

The Weight of Unspoken Words

Heavy hangs silence, like clouds full of rain,
Words left unuttered, a lingering pain.
In the hush of the night, I yearn to confide,
The weight of my thoughts, I can no longer hide.

Each moment a struggle, a battle within,
To voice all my feelings, where shall I begin?
The fear of rejection, the risk of disdain,
Keeps me imprisoned within my own brain.

The truth lingers heavy like stones in my chest,
A symphony restless, yet never expressed.
With every heartbeat, I carry this load,
The weight of unspoken words, a heavy road.

Yet hope flickers softly, a candle in hand,
To breathe out the silence, to finally stand.
With courage renewed, I'll speak from the heart,
Embrace all the feelings, let the healing start.

For every unspoken word deserves its grace,
To be freed from the shadows, to find its place.
The weight may be heavy, but love's light will soar,
In the sharing of truths, we'll create so much more.

A Room Where Laughter Faded

The walls are lined with echoes,
Memories linger like dust.
Faded photos hang in silence,
Once bright, now held by rust.

Footsteps shuffle on the floor,
Once filled with joyful cheer.
Now whispers fill the corners,
In the shadows, they disappear.

A clock ticks soft, reminders,
Of times we once held dear.
Now the laughter's just a whisper,
Lost in the empty sphere.

Sunlight seeps through the curtains,
Dancing on the chair.
But the joy that filled this room,
Has vanished in the air.

Empty glasses on the table,
Stories left untold.
The room stands still and waiting,
For memories to unfold.

Ephemeral Moments in a Seat

A chair sits by the window,
Where sunbeams softly bend.
Each moment drips like honey,
Time slips, it has no end.

The view outside keeps changing,
Seasons dance in parade.
Yet here, the heart keeps beating,
In the calm, it won't fade.

Breaths mix with the fragrance,
Of blooms that greet the sun.
In this fleeting place, I savor,
Each second, one by one.

Thoughts drift like gentle clouds,
Floating in the soft blue.
In this simple chair, I find,
Moments pure and true.

Yet shadows start to lengthen,
As day turns into night.
I linger in this seat, and
Hold on with all my might.

Lost Connections

Messages left unread,
Echoes of a past embrace.
Voices tangled in silence,
Memories start to erase.

Once vibrant talks and laughter,
Now quiet as the night.
Threads that once were woven,
Frayed ends, lost from sight.

Pictures fade on the mantle,
Time washes them away.
Promises made in fervor,
Now just words gone astray.

Reaching out for a heartbeat,
But distance grows each day.
Hands once warm in the daylight,
Now cool as skies turn gray.

Hope flickers like a candle,
In a storm that won't relent.
Yet in the heart, a whisper,
Says love is never spent.

The Silence of Togetherness

Two hearts sit side by side,
In a quiet, sacred space.
No words needed to fill,
This soft, warm embrace.

Time drips like melting candle,
Each second holds its breath.
In the stillness, we discover,
Life's meaning, even death.

Eyes meet in gentle glances,
A language all our own.
In this silence, we communicate,
Seeds of love have grown.

The world outside is rushing,
Yet here, we find our way.
In the hush, our souls entwine,
No need for words to say.

As evening's shadows deepen,
And stars begin to gleam,
In the silence of togetherness,
We weave our quiet dream.

Nooks of Nostalgia

In the corners where shadows play,
Whispers of laughter gently sway.
Old photographs in frames so small,
Capture moments that still enthrall.

A scent of pine from distant trees,
Carried on the softest breeze.
Each object tells a tale so dear,
A memory held, forever near.

The old swing creaks in twilight glow,
Where time drifts slowly, soft and slow.
Each rattle of leaves, a gentle sigh,
In these nooks where we once would lie.

Sunlight dances on the dusty floor,
Echoes of children, laughter and more.
Such simple treasures, yet they remain,
A canvas of love, joy, and pain.

As shadows stretch and daylight wanes,
A heart beats softly, love still reigns.
In every nook, a piece of heart,
In nostalgia's grip, we never part.

The Stillness of Time Forgotten

In the quiet of the evening's sigh,
Time reveals what days do lie.
Whispers float on the dusky air,
Echoes of dreams that linger there.

A clock ticks softly, not in a rush,
While shadows blend in the evening hush.
Fragments of light, a ghostly beam,
Dance across the surface, like a dream.

Each moment, a droplet in the sea,
Of stories untold, yet vivid and free.
In stillness, past and present blend,
A timeless song that will never end.

The stars awaken, one by one,
As night descends and the day is done.
In this space of calm so profound,
The pulse of existence wraps all around.

Through the years that seem to fade,
A tapestry of life is laid.
In the stillness of shadows cast,
We find the echoes of our past.

Sidelined Echoes

Among the trees where silence stands,
Lies a path touched by gentle hands.
Faded footprints tell their story,
Of moments shared in fleeting glory.

The wind whispers secrets lost in the night,
Of laughter once pooled in soft twilight.
Each corner turned holds tales untold,
In the warmth of companionship bold.

Branches sway, as if to recall,
The joy and the sorrow that comes to us all.
A rustling leaf, a distant call,
Reminds us of those we miss, stand tall.

Yet here in the hush, the heart can glean,
The vitality held in the spaces between.
For echoes may sideline, but do not erase,
The bonds that linger in time and place.

As twilight descends, with shades so fine,
We gather the moments, woven, divine.
In sidelined echoes, we stand still,
Rekindling the warmth of the heart's deep will.

The Unworn Hearth

In the heart of a home, where warmth resides,
The unworn hearth, where memory hides.
Fires once blazing now softly glow,
As stories linger in the embers' flow.

Each crackle holds a whisper shared,
Of dreams once spoken, of hearts laid bare.
The stony mantle, a steadfast friend,
Bears witness to love that will never end.

Photographs hang with smiles preserved,
In the quiet spaces, they all deserve.
Each age, each phase, a journey vast,
Rooted in the moments that forever last.

Through seasons that come and seasons that go,
The unworn hearth remains aglow.
With tales of laughter and bits of sorrow,
A promise of hope for each tomorrow.

In shadows cast by flickering light,
We gather close, hearts taking flight.
For in every fire, a story burns,
The unworn hearth, where love returns.

A Refuge of Memories

In the quiet corners of my mind,
Echoes of laughter softly unwind.
Whispers of days long past and free,
A sanctuary of what used to be.

Faded photographs, edges worn,
Stories of joy and love were born.
Each face a tale, each smile a thread,
In this refuge, the heart is fed.

Time dances slowly, a gentle glide,
With every memory, I take pride.
The warmth of hugs, the taste of bread,
Here in the moments, we never dread.

Old letters tied with a ribbon neat,
Words of affection, so bittersweet.
In this cocoon, I find my way,
The refuge of memories, night and day.

So let me dwell where shadows play,
In the vibrant hues of yesterday.
For in these dreams, my spirit flies,
In the refuge where my heart lies.

The Weight of History

Stone walls echo with tales untold,
Of battles fought, of hearts turned cold.
Each crack and crevice holds the sound,
Of voices crying from the ground.

Ancient trees, with branches wide,
Guard the secrets, where memories hide.
In their shadows, we seek to learn,
From the fires of the past, we yearn.

The ink of time, in pages stained,
Holds stories of love, of joy, of pain.
We carry forward their burdens vast,
In the weight of history, we're steadfast.

Footsteps linger on the dusty floor,
Remnants of those who came before.
Each heartbeat echoes as we tread,
In the weight of history, we're led.

With every lesson, the past unwinds,
Shaping the souls that it binds.
With reverence, we embrace the scroll,
For the weight of history shapes us whole.

Intangible Connections

Threads unseen, yet deeply felt,
In hearts entwined, emotions melt.
Silence speaks in softest tones,
An unbroken bond that we've known.

In fleeting glances, sparks ignite,
A dance of souls in the starlit night.
With whispers carried on the breeze,
Intangible connections put us at ease.

We share the laughter, the weight of tears,
A tapestry woven throughout the years.
In every heartbeat, a story spins,
Inbetween the spaces, true love begins.

Though miles may stretch, the heart knows well,
In every absence, a tale to tell.
For deep within, we understand,
Intangible connections, hand in hand.

So let us treasure, this sacred thread,
The invisible link that has been spread.
For in the quiet, our spirits roam,
In intangible connections, we find home.

Portals of the Heart

Windows open to endless skies,
Where dreams take flight, and hope never dies.
Each portal whispers secrets deep,
Guarding the treasures that we keep.

In the sunset's glow, we find our way,
Through the colors of night and day.
With every heartbeat, with every sigh,
Portals of the heart let us fly.

Moments captured in golden hues,
Lead us forward with vibrant views.
Through laughter's dance and sorrow's art,
We traverse the portals of the heart.

Behind each door, a story lies,
Of endless journeys beneath the skies.
We step with courage, never apart,
In the embrace of the heart's firm chart.

So let us explore these sacred ways,
Embrace the magic of fleeting days.
For within each portal, we find the start,
Of love's adventure through the heart.

A Reminder of Laughter

In the garden where shadows play,
Children's laughter fills the day.
Joy dances on the gentle breeze,
Echoes of life, hearts at ease.

Sunshine spills on the grassy floor,
Every giggle opens a door.
Memories painted in hues so bright,
A symphony of pure delight.

Through the window, the world may seem,
Like a forgotten or distant dream.
But in the heart, it always stays,
A reminder of those carefree days.

Laughter shared beneath the trees,
Whispers of joy that never cease.
Moments captured in golden light,
Forever cherished, forever bright.

So hold onto the joy you find,
In every heart, love intertwined.
Let laughter echo, let spirits soar,
For in our laughter, we are more.

Unheard Echoes

In the silence where whispers fade,
Lives a truth that's unafraid.
The heart echoes what it knows,
In the stillness quietly flows.

Memories linger, soft and clear,
Unseen tales they long to share.
In every shadow, a story waits,
Of lost dreams and fleeting fates.

The world spins on, yet we yearn,
For the voices that once returned.
In the echo that no one hears,
A symphony formed from our fears.

Listen closely, world so wide,
To the wisdom that we hide.
In every heart, a silent song,
A yearning for where we belong.

Though unheard, the echoes stand,
Waiting for a gentle hand.
To lift the veil, let them be,
A chorus of hope, wild and free.

Cradle of Forgotten Dreams

In a corner of a faded room,
Lie the hopes that used to bloom.
Dusty pages of open books,
Filled with wishes, tender looks.

Whispers of what could have been,
In twilight's glow, they softly spin.
Cradled safe in memory's deep,
These dreams are ours, forever keep.

Once they danced in vibrant hues,
Now they rest, in quiet blues.
Frayed edges tell their tales so sweet,
Of paths we walked, of hearts, we meet.

The cradle rocks with gentle sighs,
As forgotten hopes whisper and rise.
In the silence, they yearn for light,
To break the dawn, to take flight.

Nurtured within the soul's embrace,
Every dream has its rightful place.
In the cradle of life's embrace,
Lies the spark, our saving grace.

Beyond the Missing

In the twilight, shadows blend,
Whispers of those we cannot mend.
Yet in the heart, their essence stays,
Guiding us through the blurred days.

The stars above hold stories true,
Of love and loss, of me and you.
In every sorrow, a lesson learned,
Through every tear, a fire burned.

We walk the paths they used to tread,
With heavy hearts, yet lightly led.
Beyond the missing, we find our way,
In every night, there comes a day.

They whisper softly through the trees,
In every sigh, in every breeze.
Though distant dreams may softly fade,
Their love remains, never betrayed.

So lift your gaze to the stars above,
Feel their presence, their endless love.
For beyond the missing, we shall see,
They live within, eternally.

Echoes of Presence

In the quiet of the night,
Footsteps linger, hearts take flight.
Memories dance like shadows past,
Echoes of a love that casts.

Through the hallways, whispers roam,
Every corner feels like home.
Laughter fades into the air,
Yet I sense you lingering there.

Time stretches like a fragile thread,
Colors bleed where dreams are fed.
Fleeting moments clutch my heart,
In their warmth, we shall not part.

Beneath the stars, our secrets swell,
In twilight's hush, I know you well.
Voices softly hum our song,
In echoes, we forever belong.

When dawn arrives, the veil will lift,
Yet every wound is also a gift.
In silence, love will find its way,
An unyielding bond will always stay.

Shadows of Solitude

In twilight's glow, the shadows creep,
A solitary vigil, memories deep.
Whispers echo in the still of night,
Chasing ghosts that fade from sight.

Walls remember secrets shared,
In silence, souls have bared.
Yet in the quiet, fears arise,
Fabric woven of hopeful lies.

The moonlight casts a fleeting glance,
While dreams linger in a trance.
Loneliness holds a tender hand,
Where silence speaks, and sorrows stand.

Footsteps dance in empty halls,
Laughter muted as darkness calls.
Still, the heart clings to the light,
Amidst the shadows, holds on tight.

Through endless nights, the soul does roam,
Seeking solace, searching home.
Yet in this solitude, I'll find,
The strength to journey, undefined.

A Seat at the Table

Gather round where stories blend,
Hearts unite, and sorrows mend.
A seat awaits, pull up a chair,
In this circle, love laid bare.

The warmth of laughter fills the air,
Shared memories and gentle care.
Voices rise like a sweet refrain,
In every joy, we ease the pain.

A table set for kin and friend,
In every heart, a hand to lend.
Together we feast on dreams fulfilled,
In this haven, hope is spilled.

With every bite, we share our truth,
Like aged wine, each moment's youth.
Stories linger, woven tight,
In this gathering, pure delight.

So take your place, and do not roam,
For here you'll find your truest home.
In every sip and every cheer,
A seat at the table draws you near.

Whispers of What Was

In silent rooms where shadows blend,
Whispers float of love, my friend.
Threads of time woven with grace,
In the heart, we find our place.

Memories dance in soft caress,
Echoes linger in the blessed.
Fragments of a life we've known,
In twilight's glow, seeds are sown.

Each story told, a precious gem,
Reaching back to who, when, and them.
With every sigh, the past unfolds,
In whispers sweet, a future holds.

Remembered laughter fills the air,
In every glance, a tender stare.
What was lost is never gone,
In whispered dreams, we carry on.

And through the night, we softly tread,
With every tear, and every thread.
The past we cherish, a guiding star,
In whispers of what was, we are.

Remnants of a Laughter Lost

In shadows where we used to play,
The echoes fade, they're far away.
Once bright, our smiles began to blend,
Now silence stirs where voices end.

Faded pictures on the wall,
Remind of joy, now oh so small.
Each memory a ghostly trace,
Of laughter lost, a distant place.

We danced beneath the stars awake,
With every step, a joy we'd make.
But time, it steals with gentle hands,
And laughter fades like shifting sands.

Yet in the dark, I still recall,
The warmth of love, the dreams we'd sprawl.
Remnants linger, whispers bold,
Of laughter shared and stories told.

Hope flickers like a candle's light,
In corners dim, it burns so bright.
Though laughter's song is out of tune,
The remnants dance beneath the moon.

Solitude at the Table

A single chair against the wall,
An empty plate, once shared by all.
Fork and knife in silence rest,
Awaiting joy, a lonely guest.

The table spread with memories dear,
But absence whispers, crystal clear.
Chairs lined up, but none will stay,
Each moment drifts, then slips away.

Conversations lost to time's cruel hand,
In solitude, I make my stand.
A cup of tea, steam rising slow,
Symbols of love where none can go.

I raise my glass to shadows past,
In hopes that memories will last.
Alone I share this meal with grace,
In stillness finds a warm embrace.

Tomorrow promises a brand new sun,
Yet here, I linger, alone, but one.
Each bite a journey, bittersweet,
In solitude, my heart finds heat.

Emptiness Cradled

In a quiet room, the stillness hums,
Around me, shadows weave like drums.
A cradle rocks with empty air,
Where laughter danced, now just despair.

Hugs once wrapped like warmest blankets,
Now distant dreams and heartless skankets.
Voices fade, like whispered dreams,
Emptiness is all that seems.

I wander through this hollow space,
Looking for a familiar face.
Yet time has left me here alone,
In the echoes of a muted tone.

I hold the silence, cradle tight,
Wishing for those days of light.
But memories slip, like sand from grasp,
Emptiness cradled, time's cruel clasp.

Yet in the void, I find a spark,
A flicker bright that breaks the dark.
With every breath, I start anew,
In emptiness, hope's light shines through.

An Invitation Unanswered

A letter laid upon the floor,
Written words, a heartfelt score.
An invitation, penned with care,
Yet silence echoes in the air.

The candle flickers, shadows dance,
A moment missed, a fleeting chance.
I call your name, but no reply,
As hours drift like leaves that fly.

Each line a wish, a bridge to cross,
Yet here I stand, encased in loss.
A table set for two, not one,
An empty chair, where love once spun.

Days bleed into a weary night,
And hope retreats from fading light.
Yet still I wait, with heart in hand,
For answers lost in shifting sand.

Perhaps someday you'll find your way,
To the words I dared to say.
Until then, I'll hold this space,
An invitation, lost in grace.

The Heart's Nook

In a quiet corner, shadows play,
Whispers of love from yesterday.
Nestled soft where dreams reside,
In the heart's nook, feelings bide.

Memories dance in gentle light,
Carving paths through endless night.
Softened sighs and tender tunes,
Echo through the silent moons.

Hope like petals, fragile, clear,
Cradled close, and always near.
In the stillness, voices blend,
In the heart's nook, time won't end.

With every beat, the moments flow,
Like river streams that ebb and glow.
In warm embraces, fears dissolve,
The heart's nook, our lives evolve.

Outside the world may rush and race,
But in this space, there's gentle grace.
Wrapped in warmth, no need to roam,
In the heart's nook, we're always home.

An Invitation to Remembrance

In the garden where shadows creep,
Memories lie, both wide and deep.
Come take a stroll, hear the call,
An invitation to recall.

Petals flutter like whispered names,
Echoing love in soft refrains.
Join the dance of time gone past,
Embrace the moments that forever last.

Underneath the ancient trees,
Stories linger on the breeze.
Listen close, let silence speak,
In remembrance, find what we seek.

With every heart that beats in tune,
Olden echoes softly croon.
A tapestry of smiles and tears,
In remembrance, we conquer fears.

So take my hand, don't look away,
In this realm, let memories stay.
A gentle moment shared in grace,
An invitation to embrace.

Reflections of Tomorrow

Beneath the stars, with hope we gaze,
Counting dreams in twilight's haze.
Each reflection, a guiding spark,
Illuminating paths through dark.

Tomorrow whispers, soft and clear,
Promises held within the year.
With every breath, new chances bloom,
Turning shadows into room.

In quiet moments, futures weave,
Unfolding tales we dare believe.
From past's embrace, we learn to soar,
Reflections open every door.

So let us walk on starlit streets,
Where every step and heartbeat meets.
With eyes wide open to the dawn,
Reflections guide us, carry on.

With every sunrise, laughter rings,
As we dance with all life brings.
Bound by dreams and love's sweet glow,
In reflections, tomorrow grows.

Sheltered by Absence

In the quiet, silence speaks,
Sheltered by absence, longing leaks.
Echoes of laughter linger near,
Fragments of memories we hold dear.

Between the beats of time we stand,
Holding tight to the unseen hand.
Lost but never far away,
In absence, love finds a way.

Through the shadows, whispers sigh,
Painting pictures as days go by.
In stillness, hearts can understand,
Sheltered by absence, hand in hand.

We walk the path where shadows roam,
With every footprint, we find home.
In gentle gazes, stories weave,
Sheltered by absence, we believe.

Though distance stretches wide and far,
Love remains our guiding star.
In the heart's embrace, we find grace,
Sheltered by absence, we find place.

www.ingramcontent.com/pod-product-compliance
Ingram Content Group UK Ltd.
Pitfield, Milton Keynes, MK11 3LW, UK
UKHW031957131224
452403UK00010B/491